Joy Along the Way

Sixty-second readings that make the trip worthwhile

Steve Goodier

First Edition

Life Support System ♥ Publishing, Inc.
P.O. Box 260804 Highlands Ranch, CO 80163-0804
www.LifeSupportSystem.com

In joy,
Steve Goodier

Joy Along the Way

Sixty-second readings that make the trip worthwhile

By Steve Goodier

Life Support System♡Publishing, Inc.
P.O. Box 260804 Highlands Ranch, CO 80163-0804

Library of Congress Card Number: 00-190313

ISBN 1-929664-02-8 (Softcover)

Cover design: Brent Stewart & Darrel Voth

Contents

Glimpses of Greatness

Greatness is too often defined by an unusual act of courage or a life of extraordinary merit or virtue. But glimpses of greatness can be seen all around us, and especially in those who genuinely care for others.

Father Albert Braun was such a man. After his ordination, he requested to live amongst some of the poorest of the world's poor. He was sent to the Mescalero Apache reservation in south central New Mexico (USA). Father Braun learned to love the Apache. And as he lived with them, he learned from them and they learned from him. They became family.

He stayed many years on the reservation but left it twice to serve as a chaplain during both World Wars. He almost died in World War II when his Allied forces tried to defend the Philippine Islands from attack. Many of his comrades died during the fighting and Father Braun risked his own life to comfort the wounded and give the dying Last Rites. He was forced to march with no food and little water. Along the way, many more of the men died. And in the prisoner of war camps, more lives yet were lost to disease, cruel physical treatment and malnutrition.

Father Braun had learned much from the Apache about surviving off the land. When he went out on work detail, he found fruit and edible vegetables which he smuggled back into the camp to help supplement the men's diets. Once he acquired the vaccine for diphtheria which he also secreted into camp, but it wasn't enough. They drew lots to determine who would get the medicine. Though afflicted himself, he gave his portion to a young soldier. Before long, he suffered simultaneously from diphtheria, malaria, dysentery and beriberi.

He barely survived. After the war he asked to be returned to New Mexico to live once again with the Apache. When he knew that his own death was near, Father Braun requested to be buried on the reservation, surrounded by his Apache "family."

Today, at the church of St. Joseph, one can see portraits of the Apache's greatest chiefs and warriors. There is a portrait of Geronimo, one of Cochise, a picture of Victorio and a portrait of Father Albert Braun, who came to live among them as a true friend.

Father Braun showed a certain greatness, not by any one heroic deed, but by the sum total of a life of caring. Such glimpses of greatness can be seen shining from the hearts of all who care.

Time to Be Quiet

Popular author and speaker Ken Blanchard sometimes tells a powerful story about Red, a corporate president who, as a young man, learned an important and life-changing lesson. Red had just graduated from college and was offered an opportunity to interview for a position with a firm in New York City. As the job involved moving his wife and small child from Texas to New York, he wanted to talk the decision over with someone before accepting it, but his father had died and Red did not feel he had anybody to turn to. On impulse, he telephoned an old friend of the family, someone his father had suggested he turn to if he ever needed good advice.

The friend said he would be happy to give Red advice about the job offer under the condition that the young man *take* whatever advice he was given. "You might want to think about that for a couple of days before hearing my suggestion," he was told.

Two days later Red called the man back and said he was ready to listen to his counsel. "Go on to New York City and have the interview," the older man said. "But I want you to go up there in a very special way. I want you to go on a train and I want you to get a private compartment. Don't take anything to write with, anything to listen to or anything to read, and don't talk to anybody except to put in your order for dinner with the porter. When you get to New York call me and I will tell you what to do next."

Red followed the advice precisely. The trip took two days. As he had brought along nothing to do and kept entirely to himself, he quickly became bored. It soon dawned on him what was happening. He was being forced into quiet time. He could do nothing but think and meditate. About three hours outside New York City he broke the rules and asked for a pencil and paper. Until the train stopped, he wrote -- the culmination of all his meditation.

Red called the family friend from the train station. "I know what you wanted," he said. "You wanted me to think. And now I know what to do. I don't need anymore help."

"I didn't think you would, Red," came the reply. "Good luck."

Now, years later, Red heads a corporation in California. And he has always made it a policy to take a couple of days to be alone. He goes where there is no phone, no television and no people. He goes to be alone; to meditate and to listen.

Andre Gide reminds us to "be faithful to that which exists within yourself." The answers you seek may be very close indeed.

P.S.

It is accurately said that "there is always music amongst the trees in the garden, but our hearts must be very quiet to hear it."
~ M. Aumonier

Millennium Dream

The daughter of comedian Groucho Marx was once denied admittance to an exclusive country club swimming pool with her friends because she and her family were not members. Realizing what had happened, embarrassed officials sent the Marx family an apology and an application to join. Groucho declined the invitation with the comment, "I wouldn't want to belong to any club that would have me as a member."

Someone still tried to smooth over the incident by persuading the comedian to allow an application to be submitted for membership. The country club was embarrassed further when the application was denied. The reason? The Marx family was Jewish and the club was "restricted."

True to form, Groucho wrote back: "My wife is not Jewish. Can she go swimming and let our daughter wade up to her waist?"

I love his use of humor, but Groucho effectively shines a spotlight on the prevalence and absurdity of prejudice. He must have felt, as did Sir Isaac Newton so many years earlier, that we "build too many walls and not enough bridges."

I yearn for a time when we courageously break down those walls that divide and build wide bridges between one another. I long for a super-highway of compassion and acceptance spanning our differences to unite all humanity as one. At the dawn of the new millennium I dream of an age when people will be finally connected heart to heart and mind to mind.

And I will do what I can to build bridges. Will you join me?

Sitting On Your Talent

If you are like me, there are some things you may feel you do pretty well, and others that you would not admit to having done even at gunpoint! Please don't expect anything I build with my hands to remain standing past sundown, or anything I attempt to repair to ever stay fixed after I leave the room. And if my cars relied solely on me to keep them going, I would walk most everywhere I go.

On the other hand, I do play guitar adequately and I can make a memorable enchilada dish. I also enjoy working with people and I seem to have made it a lifelong project to learn how to become a better listener.

I never thought of myself as one who has any great talent, but like each of us, I have certain skills and abilities. Let me tell you a story, however, I once heard speaker Les Brown relate. It's a story about a man who had *real* talent.

This particular man played piano in a bar. He was a good piano player. People came out just to hear him and his trio play. But one night, a patron wanted them to sing a particular song. The trio didn't sing much and declined.

But the customer was persistent. He told the bartender, "I'm tired of listening to the piano. I want that guy to sing!"

The bartender shouted across the room, "Hey buddy! If you want to get paid, sing the song. The patrons are asking you to sing!"

So he did. He sang a song. A jazz piano player who had never sung the song in public did so for the very first time. And nobody had ever heard *Sweet Lorraine* sung the way it was sung that night by Nat King Cole!

He had talent he was sitting on! He may have lived the rest of his life playing in a jazz trio in no-name bars, but because he *had* to sing, he went on to become one of the best-known entertainers in America.

You, too, have skills and abilities. You may not feel as if your "talent" is particularly great, but it may be better than you think! And with persistence, most skills can be improved. Besides, you may as well have no ability at all if you sit on whatever talent you possess!

Some people ask, "What ability do I have that is useful?" Others ask, "How will I use the ability that I have?"

P.S.

Speaking of ability, one person says, "I'm multi-talented: I can talk and annoy you at the same time!"

Are You Ready?

In her book *Teaching a Stone to Talk* (New York: Harper Collins, 1988), Annie Dillard reveals a sad, but poignant story about what happens when we set out unprepared. She tells of a British Arctic expedition which set sail in 1845 to chart the Northwest Passage around the Canadian Arctic to the Pacific Ocean. Neither of the two ships and none of the 138 men aboard returned.

Captain Sir John Franklin prepared as if they were embarking on a pleasure cruise rather than an arduous and grueling journey through one of earth's most hostile environments. He packed a 1,200 volume library, a hand-organ, china place settings for officers and men, cut-glass wine goblets and sterling silver flatware, beautifully and intricately designed. Years later, some of these place settings would be found near a clump of frozen, cannibalized bodies.

The voyage was doomed when the ships sailed into frigid waters and became trapped in ice. First ice coated the decks, the spars and the rigging. Then water froze around the rudders, and the ships became hopelessly locked in the now-frozen sea.

Sailors set out to search for help (possibly delirious from lead-poisoning from the cans which preserved their food), but soon succumbed to severe Arctic weather and died of exposure to its harsh winds and subfreezing temperatures. For the next twenty years, remains of the expedition were found all over the frozen landscape.

The crew did not prepare either for the cold or for the eventuality of the ships becoming ice-locked. On a voyage which was to last two to three years, they packed only their Navy-issue uniforms and the captain carried just a 12-day supply of coal for the auxiliary steam engines. The frozen body of an officer was eventually found, miles from the vessel, wearing his uniform of fine blue cloth, edged with silk braid, a blue greatcoat and a silk neckerchief -- clothing which was noble and respectful, but wholly inadequate.

Historians may doubt the wisdom of such an ill-prepared journey. But more important for us is the question, are we, too, prepared for the lengthy voyage we've embarked upon, that journey we call "life"? Have we made ourselves ready for all that will surely await us? Physically and mentally, are we prepared to handle what may come? Do we regularly stay fit through daily study and exercise? Will our minds and bodies be ready to cope with challenges which will surely arise?

Emotionally and spiritually, are we ready? Do we practice such virtues as love, joy, peace, patience, kindness, gentleness, faithfulness, goodness and self-control? Will we be emotionally and spiritually ready to embrace an unknown future?

To embark on a journey unprepared can set us up for disastrous results. But the good news is, we can still prepare for ours. And in large part, the success of our voyage will be determined by our regular and systematic preparation.

Are you ready?

Room in the Bank

Is your life full and busy? Perhaps, *too* busy? Sometimes we fill our lives so full we don't have time for the important things. At such times I remember a story about a young girl and her bank.

The little girl's father had just given her a silver dollar to put into her bank. She excitedly ran off to her room to "deposit" the coin. However, in a few minutes she returned and handed the silver coin back to her father.

"Daddy," she said sadly, "here's your dollar back. I can't get it into my bank."

"Why not?" her concerned father asked.

"It's too full," she said, obviously disappointed.

Her father accompanied her back to her room and, sure enough, her bank was too full to accept even one more coin. It was filled with pennies!

Sometimes our lives are like that bank. So full of errands, obligations and activities that neither nurture us nor help anyone else, that there simply is no room left for what is truly important -- the silver dollars.

Grenville Kleiser has said, "To live at this time is an inestimable privilege, and a sacred obligation devolves upon you to make right use of your opportunities. Today is the day in which to attempt and achieve something worthwhile."

Have you made room for any large coins in your bank; for those things you believe to be worthwhile? If not, you may have to remove a few pennies, but I suspect you will never know they are gone!

P.S.

As one philosopher says, "Evaporation gets blamed for a lot of things people forget to put the top on."

Bluebird of Happiness

A sign in a pet store read, "If anybody has seen the Bluebird of Happiness, would you please notify this pet store?"

Happiness seems to be in short supply for many people. If the results of recent surveys can be trusted, there is a general decline of happiness in today's world. And people were not all that cheerful a few years back! It was Oliver Wendell Holmes who stated, "I might have been a minister for aught I know, if a certain clergyman had not looked and talked like an undertaker." (I have to say, though, that some clergy and undertakers I've known could teach the rest of us something about joy!)

Joy and happiness are not always the same things. Happiness can be thought of as more of a temporary, emotional condition, often based on outside circumstances. Joy, on the other hand, is deeper. We can be basically joyful, regardless of a particular unhappy situation that we may be enduring. It is often just a matter of keeping perspective on our troubles, and especially when those troubles seem to be in long supply.

You may know the story of the man who had a marvelous way of keeping joy in his life. He was a carpenter. He followed the same ritual every day when he came home from the job. He stopped by a small tree in his front yard and placed his hand on a couple of branches. Then, when he walked into his home, it was as if a magical transformation had occurred. All of a sudden, the stress was lifted from him. He became energetic and joyful, able to fully interact with his children and his wife.

He explained it this way: "That tree is my trouble tree. When I come home I stop by the tree and, just like I leave my tools in the truck, I leave my troubles outside of my home. I hang them on that tree before greeting my family. Anything that does not have to come in my house stays outside. Anything which I do not have to deal with at home, I leave on that tree. And in the morning, I stop by the tree and pick up the troubles I left there in the evening."

Then he adds, "It's a funny thing, though. Every morning I always find fewer troubles hanging there than I remembered the night before."

Here is a man who has no doubt seen the Bluebird of Happiness. Chances are, it is nesting in a tree just outside his home!

There is wisdom in knowing that some problems can wait until tomorrow. And more wisdom in knowing what to hang on the tree and what to bring in. Managing daily problems well is vital to maintaining joy.

Early to Bed

Some people are fortunate enough to be able to do what they love. But not everyone can follow their bliss into the job market. For some people, the motto, "Early to bed and early to rise, 'till you make enough money to do otherwise," fits better. These others have to make the decision to love what they do, since they do not find themselves doing what they love.

It also stands to reason that the more we enjoy our work, the more successful we will likely become. And usually we will make more money!

An employee went to his supervisor to ask for a raise. "I am already planning on giving you a raise," she said.

"Oh, great!" he said. "When will it be effective?"

"As soon as you are!" shouted the boss. Ouch...

Have you noticed that effective and successful workers are those who are doing what they love and loving what they do?

I believe it was the mystic Kahil Gibran who put it this way: "Work is love made visible. And if you cannot work with love, but only with distaste, it is better that you should leave your work and sit at the gate of the temple and ask for alms of those who work with joy."

We may not need to do what we love all the time if we can learn to enjoy what we do more of the time.

P.S.

One person has a different point of view. She says, "The trouble with work is -- it's so daily."

Just in Time

Do you ever worry about what *might* happen in the future? Or do you find yourself anxious about things over which you have no control? If so, then a teaching from author and lecturer Corrie ten Boom may help.

She learned a powerful lesson as a little girl. Havingencountered the cold, lifeless body of a baby, she realized that the reality of death would someday strike her family, too. Perhaps her father or mother or sister, Betsy, would soon die.

She anxiously worried about these possibilities until her father came in one night to tuck her into bed. Corrie burst into tears and sobbed, "I *need* you. You *can't* die. You *can't!*"

Her father sat on the edge of the narrow bed and spoke tenderly to his daughter. "Corrie," he said gently, "when you and I go to Amsterdam, when do I give you your ticket?"

She sniffed a few times and considered the question. "Why, just before I get on the train," she answered.

"Exactly," he continued. Then he gave her assurance that was to last a lifetime. He told her that a wise God knows when she will need things, too.

"Don't run out ahead of God," he cautioned her. "When the time comes that some of us have to die, you will look into your heart and find the strength you need -- just in time."

Corrie and her family were sent to concentration camps where she suffered greatly during World War II. She, indeed, was to experience the deaths of her parents and sister, as well as numerous friends. She was to endure hardships which she could never have imagined as a young child. But the words of her father stayed with her and proved to be true. "You will look into your heart and find the strength you need -- just in time." Regardless of the suffering or hardship she encountered, when she looked inside her heart she found the strength she needed -- just in time.

If you find yourself worried or anxious about an uncertain future...perhaps you are running ahead. You have not yet been given the ticket for the journey. And if that thing you fear should ever arrive, it is then you must look inside your heart. The strength you need can be found there -- just in time.

Follow Your Bliss

Author Joseph Campbell often talked about "following your bliss." I heard of a bus driver in Chicago who does just that.

He sings while he drives. That's right... *sings!* And I don't mean he sings softly to himself, either. He sings so that the whole bus can hear! All day long he drives and sings.

He was once interviewed on Chicago television. He said that he is not actually a bus driver. "I'm a professional singer," he asserted. "I only drive the bus to get a captive audience every single day."

His "bliss" is not driving a bus, though that may be a source of enjoyment for some people. His bliss is singing. And the supervisors at the Chicago Transit Authority are perfectly happy about the whole arrangement. You see, people line up to ride his bus. They even let other busses pass by so they can ride with the "singing bus driver." They love it!

Here is a man who believes he knows why he was put here on earth. For him, it is to make people happy. And the more he sings, the more people he makes happy! He has found a way to align his purpose in living with his occupation. By following his bliss, he is actually living the kind of life he believes he was meant to live.

Not everybody can identify a purpose in life. But when you do, and when you pursue it, you will be living the kind of life you feel you were meant to live. And what's more, you will be happy.

P.S.

I believe it was Mark Twain who said, "The good Lord didn't create anything without a purpose, but the fly comes close."

The World's Most Communicative Disease

There is a story in circulation about an optimistic farmer who couldn't wait to greet each new day with a resounding, "Good morning, God!" He lived near a woman whose morning greeting was more like, "Good God. Morning?" They were each a trial to the other. Where he saw opportunity, she saw problems. What brought him satisfaction, brought her discontentment.

One bright morning he exclaimed, "Look at the beautiful sky! Did you ever see such a glorious sunrise?"

"Yeah," she countered. "It'll probably get so hot the crops will scorch!"

During an afternoon shower, he commented, "Isn't this wonderful? Mother Nature is giving the corn a drink today!"

"And if it doesn't stop before too long," came the sour reply, "we'll wish we'd taken out flood insurance on the crops!" And so it went.

Convinced that he could instill some awe and wonder in this hardened woman, he bought a remarkable dog. Not just any mutt, but the most expensive, highly trained and gifted dog he could find. The animal was exquisite! It could perform remarkable and impossible feats which, the farmer thought, would surely amaze even his neighbor. So he invited her to watch his dog perform.

"Fetch!" he commanded, as he tossed a stick into a lake, where it bobbed up and down in the rippling water. The dog bounded after the stick, walked *on* the water, and retrieved it.

"What do you think of that?" he asked, smiling.

"Hmmm," she frowned. "Can't swim, can he?"

I believe that attitudes are the world's most communicative diseases. They can be as catching as any known virus. And when negative and cynical, they can be just as deadly.

But a stubbornly positive attitude can often make the difference between happiness and misery, between health and illness and even between life and death. Once infected, you'll never be the same.

Shot of Enthusiasm

Enthusiasm is something I can get excited about!

I remember a story told about playwright and U.S. Ambassador to Italy, Claire Booth Luce. She became a Roman Catholic late in life and, like many others converted to something new, she seemed to possess limitless enthusiasm and energy about her new faith.

A reporter once spotted her engrossed in deep conversation with the pope. He crept within earshot, all the while wondering what important issues the ambassador and the pope could be discussing. Finally, he was close enough to hear the pope say to Ms. Luce, "But I already *am* a Catholic!"

All right, maybe she got carried away at times. But is it possible to be whole and happy without enthusiasm? I find that a genuine verve for living is a by-product of an unwavering focus upon that which is great and magnificent and beautiful. It is like energy pulsing forth from one who, in a positive way, is obsessed by a greater truth, a more beautiful dream, a more captivating vision.

Likewise, genuine enthusiasm attracts people. As insects are drawn to light, others are drawn to your energy and vitality. People feel alive around people who *are* alive! And the very ones drawn to you will likely be those to finally help you achieve those beautiful dreams which have hold of your heart.

Now, that's something to get excited about!

P.S.

"The greatest discovery of my generation,"
said psychologist William James, "is that
human beings can alter their lives by alter-
ing their attitudes of mind."

Hit Over the Head

In her wise and sensitive audio *Lessons in Living* (BDD Audio, 1997), Susan Taylor tells of lessons learned from experiencing a California earthquake. She was in bed in the early hours of the morning when an earthquake struck. As her house shook, she tumbled from her bed. She managed to stand underneath an arched doorway in her hall and watched in horror as her whole home literally tumbled down around her. Where her bed had once stood, she later discovered nothing but a pile of rubble. She lost everything -- every button, every dish, her automobile, every stitch of clothing.

Susan huddled, scared and crying, in the darkness of her house. It was very early in the morning and the sun had not yet risen. She began to call out for help. Crying and calling.

As exhaustion set in, she thought that maybe she should be listening for rescuers rather than calling out. She grew still and listened. In the silence around her, the only sound she heard was the beating of her own heart. It occurred to her then that at least she was still alive! She was unhurt except for cuts and bruises. She may have lost everything else, but not her life! As she thought about her situation, she was flooded with a feeling of indescribable peace and happiness, the likes of which she had never known. That experience, by the way, was to permanently change her.

In the deepest part of her being, Susan knew she had nothing to fear *whether or not she was ever rescued.* For the first time, she realized that her true security lay deep within and did not depend upon anything material -- even her physical safety!

Later, she heard sirens and voices of people calling out to her. They had found her. And this is what she says:

"Before the quake I had all the trappings of success, but my life was out of balance. I wasn't happy because I was clinging to things in my life and always wanting more. My home, my job, my clothes, a relationship -- I thought they were my security. It took an earthquake and losing everything I owned for me to discover that my security had been with me all along."

She adds, "There's a power within us that we can depend upon no matter what is happening around us. Now, each day of my life I take time to sit in silence and allow God to be God in me."

It's as if life sometimes has to hit us over the head to get our attention! But when we realize where to find true security, then we know also where to find peace.

Your Resilient Self

I often come back to a story about two men who came from similar backgrounds. They both grew up in "dysfunctional" homes. They were both raised by an alcohol-addicted parent. They both endured numerous hardships as a result of the many problems brought about by their unstable home lives.

As adults, however, their lives looked quite different. One man held a steady job. He was married with a happy home life. He was involved in his children's lives. He felt productive and useful.

A reporter interviewed him as part of an article she was writing on the effects of alcoholism in the home. "To what do you attribute your present circumstances?" she asked him, referring to his obvious success.

"Given my background," he replied, "what do you expect?"

The other man could not seem to keep a job for long. He was frequently let go for alcohol-related problems. He had been married, but lost his wife due to his addiction. He felt hopeless and believed himself to be a failure.

The reporter also asked him, "To what do you attribute your present circumstances?"

"Given my background," he replied, "what do you expect?"

Naturally, our past will shape our present. Our backgrounds are crucial in determining the kinds of decisions we will make as adults. But here is a case in which similar upbringings produced quite different results.

Both men were shaped by their past. One slipped into those old, familiar patterns and recreated them as an adult. The other was determined never to repeat what he had experienced as a child. The first man felt helpless to change. The other used his background as motivation to make needed changes.

In his book *The Resilient Self* (New York: Villard Books, 1992), Stephen Wolin emphasizes how our difficult backgrounds can actually make us more resilient. Hardships can make us strong and give us needed motivation to be different in the future. A difficult background can be no less than a marvelous gift!

For some, their background is an excuse. For others, it is a gift!

P.S.

On an unrelated note, it's been said, "Before criticizing someone, walk a mile in their shoes; then when you do criticize them, you will be a mile away and have their shoes."

When We Need Love the Most

A university instructor posed a riddle to her graduate education class. "What has four legs and leaves?" she asked, hoping the students would realize that by considering alternative meanings to the words "legs" and "leaves" that they could arrive at the solution -- a table. However, one woman unexpectedly answered, "My last two boyfriends." Maybe you can relate.

People will leave relationships for any number of reasons and sometimes they should, for not every friendship has a healthy future. Some well-intentioned people come together in heat and passion and all that is left of the union when the fire goes out is a pile of ashes. Others bring along so many destructive problems and behaviors that a happy relationship has no chance of long-term survival.

But what about when friends, lovers or family bolt from the relationship at just the wrong time? After all, those we want to love are not always "lovable" or easy to get along with! Is a temporary lapse into craziness reason enough to run?

Author John Gray sometimes tells about a young mother who asked her visiting brother to get her some pain pills. He forgot and, when her husband returned home, she was upset and in pain -- more than a bit crazy. He experienced her anger as a personal assault and exploded in defense. They exchanged harsh words and he headed for the door.

His wife said, "Stop, don't leave. This is when I need you the most! I'm in pain. I've had no sleep. Please listen. You are a fair-weather friend. If I'm sweet, you're okay; but if I'm not, out you go!" And then tearfully, and more subdued, she said, "I'm in pain. I have nothing to give. Please hold me. Don't speak...just hold me." He held her and neither spoke -- until she thanked him for being there.

It is easy to love those who are at their best. But it is during those times we are unlovable that we may need love the most. And what a beautiful thing when we get it. And even more beautiful when we find the grace to give it.

When Is Quitting Time?

Newspapers once reported about a young Taiwanese man who wrote 700 love letters to his girlfriend in a two-year period. At least two letters a day! Seven hundred letters telling of his undying love for her and encouraging her to accept his marriage proposal.

Two years of sending letters got results. She announced her engagement...to the postal worker who delivered all those letters! (I suppose she just became accustomed to his face.) Lucky for the mail carrier that her boyfriend didn't give up too soon!

There may be a time to give up, but there is certainly a time to persist. My kids, for instance, often wanted to give up music lessons. We encouraged them not to quit. "Stay with the lessons," I told them.

I have spoken with many adults who have said, "I used to take music lessons when I was a child. I regret the fact that I quit too soon. I wish I knew how to play the piano today."

I have never talked with an adult who said, "I took music lessons when I was a child. I regret the fact that I didn't quit sooner!"

Of course, it's not about music lessons...it's about knowing when to stay with something and knowing when to quit. How many books were never written because someone quit too soon? How many relationships died prematurely and how many dreams never came to fruition because someone gave them up?

Maybe it's not yet quitting time.

P.S.

Someone said, "Forgiveness is me giving up my right to hurt you for hurting me."

Letting Go of Resentments

A story tells of a merchant in a small town who had identical twin sons. The boys worked for their father in the department store he owned and, when he died, they took over the store.

Everything went well until the day a dollar bill disappeared. One of the brothers had left the bill on the cash register and walked outside with a customer. When he returned, the money was gone.

He asked his brother, "Did you see that dollar bill on the cash register?" His brother replied that he had not. But the young man kept probing and questioning. He would not let it alone. "Dollar bills just don't get up and walk away! Surely you must have seen it!" There was subtle accusation in his voice. Tempers began to rise. Resentment set in. Before long, a deep and bitter chasm divided the young men. They refused to speak. They finally decided they could no longer work together and a dividing wall was built down the center of the store. For twenty years hostility and bitterness grew, spreading to their families and to the community.

Then one day a man in an automobile licensed in another state stopped in front of the store.

He walked in and asked the clerk, "How long have you been here?"

The clerk replied that he'd been there all his life. The customer said, "I must share something with you. Twenty years ago I was 'riding the rails' and came into this town in a boxcar. I hadn't eaten for three days. I came into this store from the back door and saw a dollar bill on the cash register. I put it in my pocket and walked out. All these years I haven't been able to forget that. I know it wasn't much money, but I had to come back and ask your forgiveness."

The stranger was amazed to see tears well up in the eyes of this middle-aged man. "Would you please go next door and tell that same story to the man in the store?" he said. Then the man was even more amazed to see two middle-aged men, who looked very much alike, embracing each other and weeping together in the front of the store.

After twenty years, the brokenness was mended. The wall of resentment that divided them came down.

It is so often the little things -- like resentments -- that finally divide people. And the solution, of course, is to let them go. There is really nothing particularly profound about it. But for fulfilling and lasting relationships, letting them go is a must. Refuse to carry around bitterness and you may be surprised at how much energy you have left for building bonds with those you love.

Thanks for the Misery!

Some stories can stand dusting off. Like the one about a grandmother who took her little grandson to the beach. They were having a good time until a huge wave came in and swept the boy out to sea. She fell down on her knees and pleaded to the heavens, "Please return my grandson -- that's all I ask! *Please!!!*"

A moment later, lo and behold, a wave swelled from the ocean and deposited the wet, yet unhurt, child at her feet. She checked him over to make sure that he was okay. He was fine. But still she looked up to the heavens angrily and said, "When we came he had a hat!"

We expect her to give thanks for this extraordinary thing which happened. We're taught to show appreciation for that special act of kindness or consideration which is given. Yet, can we also say thanks when all is not so well? And better yet, should we?

A few years ago, someone stole my wife's purse. In the hassle of going about the business of helping her to replace lost cards and identification, I recalled the words of author Matthew Henry. Henry, too, was robbed. Yet he found the grace to give thanks about his situation. He said, "I give thanks that I have never been robbed before; that although he took my wallet, he did not take my life; that although he took everything, it was not much; and finally, that it was I who was robbed and not I who robbed."

He may as well have said, "Thanks for the misery!" Except that Henry was not miserable. After all, it is difficult to feel miserable when we are busy giving thanks.

P.S.

Speaking of suffering, Carol Leifer says, "I'm not into working out. My philosophy: No pain, no pain."

Standing on the Cat's Tail

A mother heard the family cat yowl in pain. She knew where to look -- she looked for her son, Mike. "Stop pulling the cat's tail, Michael!" she chided.

"I'm not pulling his tail," the boy retorted. "I'm just standing on it. He's doing the pulling."

He, of course, is no different than any of us when we want to blame someone or something else for our problems. It's the cat's fault. Or the government. Or the school. Or...

In her audio program *How Could You Do That?* (Harper Audio, 1996), Laura Schlesinger relates a story of a 40-year-old woman who was jogging along in a state park when she was attacked and killed by a mountain lion. Her family immediately filed suit against the state because of the state's "failure to manage the mountain lion population" and because it didn't "react to reports of cougar activity in the area by posting warning signs."

Interestingly, her husband dropped the suit a little later. "Barbara and I have always taken responsibility for our own actions," he explained. "Barbara chose to run in the wild and, on a very long shot, she did not come back. This is not the fault of the state, and people should take responsibility for themselves."

It is rare that we hear a story like that! I find that most of the good parts of my life, as well as those which are not all that good, are a direct result of my own decisions! When I recognize that I am ultimately responsible for the great majority of what happens to me, I begin to look for solutions to solve my problems instead of targets to blame them on. I am happier and healthier.

Taking responsibility is one more step in building a life that matters.

Ain't What I Used to Be

It has been said, "Be contented with what you have, but never too contented with what you are."

There is a story that comes out of Asia about a farmer who saw a tiger's tail swishing between two large rocks. In a moment of haste, he grabbed the tail and pulled. All of a sudden he realized he had an angry tiger by the tail and only two rocks stood between him and the tiger's teeth and claws! So there he remained, afraid to loosen his grip on the enraged animal's tail lest he surely be killed.

A monk happened by and the farmer called out in desperation, "Come over here and help me kill this tiger!"

The holy man said, "On, no. I cannot do that. I cannot take the life of another." Then he went on to deliver a homily against killing. All the while, the farmer was holding tightly to the tail of an angry tiger.

When the monk finally finished his sermon, the farmer pleaded, "If you won't kill the tiger, then at least come hold its tail while I kill it."

The monk thought that perhaps it would be all right to simply hold the tiger's tail, so he grabbed hold and pulled. The farmer, however, turned and walked away down the road.

The monk shouted after him, "Come back here and kill the tiger!"

"Oh, no," the farmer replied. "You have converted me!"

Conversion is nothing more than change. With money, conversion can be the change of a bill into coin or the change of the currency of one country into the currency of another. On the human level, conversion can be a change in beliefs, a change in ideas, a change in attitudes, a change in behaviors or a change in priorities. If the largest room in the world is "room for improvement," then it is good to leave plenty of room for change.

I like the old southern American slave's prayer: "O God, I ain't what I ought to be and I ain't what I'm a-goin' to be. But thanks to you, I ain't what I used to be!"

Here is a person who is traveling an exciting adventure! A life of change! A life of growth! And always leaving room for improvement.

It's the only way to travel.

Faces of Love

Milton Berle once quipped that "all the world loves a lover -- except people who are waiting to use the phone."

Love has many faces. The faces we see so often are ones of infatuation and romance. We speak of "falling in love" and feel, too, as if we are in free fall. But the face of love I appreciate the most is not romance, as much as I am drawn to it, but one I can always count on to be there. It is the face of devotion.

I see that face in the couple who were engaging in a dinner time disagreement. To the children's amazement, their father jumped up from the table, grabbed two sheets of paper, and said to his wife, "Let's make a list of everything we don't like about each other."

She agreed and proceeded to write. He, meanwhile, sat and glowered. She looked up and he began to write. When she continued listing complaints, he stared across the table at her. Again, when she looked up he put pen to paper and continued writing. He stopped to watch her, and every time she caught his eye, he wrote again.

They finally finished. "Let's exchange complaints," he said. They gave each other their lists.

She glanced at his sheet and pleaded, "Give mine back!" All down his sheet he had written: "I love you, I love you, I love you." Their children have always remembered that moment with humor and fondness.

As much as I enjoy romance, it's an unwavering devotion that I need the most. I need to know that love which says, "I will be with you through it all." It is a face which can often be seen on parents and grandparents, on spouses, and even on very good friends. And it is a face which, when I gaze closely enough, I can see in it something of the face of God.

If you haven't noticed that face lately, look closely. You might be surprised where you find it!

P.S.

Concerning love, eight-year-old Dave said, "Love will find you. Even if you hide from it. I have been trying to hide from it since I was five, but the girls keep finding me."

Set Your Own Agenda

Have you ever heard of Hank Greenberg? The year was 1934. For the first time in 25 years, the Detroit Tigers were a strong team who had an excellent chance to play in baseball's prestigious World Series. Hank was a key player on a team that had come to rely on his superb skills at first base, and his strong batting, to win games. An important and decisive game was scheduled on Yom Kippur. Hank, the son of Romanian immigrants to the United States, announced that he would not don his uniform and play on this day, the most sacred of Hebrew fasts.

The city of Detroit was outraged. Citizens screamed that the Day of Atonement could be celebrated any year, but this year the Tigers may go all the way to the Series! Anti-Semitic remarks were viciously hurled, but Hank Greenberg remained resolute.

The Detroit Tigers indeed lost that day, although the team did secure the pennant that year. And Hank, when more rational minds prevailed, attained the respect of the community. In fact, a poem was written and published honoring the man who

held steadfastly to his beliefs. The tribute ended
with this verse:

> *Came Yom Kippur -- Holy fast day*
> *world-wide over to the Jews,*
> *And Hank Greenberg to his teaching*
> *and the old tradition true*
> *Spent the day among his people*
> *and he didn't come to play.*
> *Said Murphy to Mulrooney,*
> *"We shall lose the game today!*
> *We shall miss him in the infield*
> *and shall miss him at the bat,*
> *But he's true to his religion --*
> *and I honor him for that!"*

Hank still teaches us an important lesson in
how to live effectively. He decided what was important to him and, regardless of pressure applied, he
honored his own values. Hank Greenberg -- not the
team, nor the coaches, nor even emotional Detroit
fans -- set his agenda. He let nobody lower stand-
ards he had chosen for himself. And though the
team lost that day, the city of Detroit won because it
gained an important role model in a young man who
courageously followed an inner voice.

Choosing our own way may not always be
easy. But effective living occurs once we decide
how we will live our lives and, regardless of outside
pressure, we honor that decision.

If you are struggling with a difficult decision today, what is your inner voice leading you to do? Perhaps that is the voice which should be honored.

In the Spin Cycle

An old story tells of a little boy who went into a grocery store and asked for extra strength laundry detergent. As the clerk was finding it, he asked the boy what he wanted to use it for. He said he wanted to give his pet rat a bath.

The clerk replied, "Well, I think that this detergent is a bit strong for a rat. I'm not sure that I would use it."

The child said that he believed it would be all right and the grocer added, "Just be careful. This is awfully strong detergent."

About a week later, the boy came back. When asked by the grocer how his rat was, he said, "It died."

"I'm sorry to hear that," sympathized the clerk. "But I did tell you that the detergent was probably too strong."

"Oh, I really don't think it was the detergent," the boy replied. "I believe it was the spin cycle that did it."

Do you ever feel as if you have been through the spin cycle? Maybe even hung out to dry? Living through pain and suffering is like going through the spin cycle. Often our pain is physical, the result of illness or injury. But more often we suffer from emotional pain like loss, fear, worry, rejection, loneliness, guilt or depression. In either case, sometimes we feel as if we have been through the spin cycle.

We sometimes long for a world with no pain, no problems, no obstacles, no disappointments, no hurts, no handicaps, no troubles. We wish our bodies might always run like fine-tuned machines -- no permanent breakdowns, no serious illness -- purring along forever, or at least until they quickly and painlessly cease to function altogether (and, of course, at the time of our choosing). We might crave a world where loss is unknown, loneliness unheard of and all things unpleasant somehow banished.

But the truth is, we live in a world with pain. And we all experience our share. We can run, but we can't hide from suffering. It will always find us. And should we even try to run from it? For even hardships may serve a valuable purpose.

Helen Keller, without sight or hearing, suffered her share of pain. But after many years of anger and hostility toward her "solitary confinement," she was eventually able to say, "I thank God *for* my handicaps. For through them, I have found myself, my work and my God."

Even for her, the suffering was worth it.

P.S.

It has been said that we take on the strength of that which we overcome.

Getting What You Deserve

According to Alan Loy McGinnis in his book *Confidence* (Minneapolis: Augsburg), actor Sidney Poitier achieved prominence in his field largely because of self reliance he learned from his parents. "I was the product of a colonial system," says Poitier, "that was very damaging to the psyche of non-white people. The darker you were, the less opportunities were presented to you."

He continues, "My parents were terribly, terribly poor, and after awhile the psychology of poverty begins to mess with your head. As a result, I cultivated a fierce pride in myself, something that was hammered into me by my parents, Evelyn and Reggie -- mostly by Evelyn. She never apologized for the fact she had to make my pants out of flour sacks. I got used to 'Imperial Flour' written across my rear. She always used to say, 'If it's clean, that's the important thing.' So from that woman -- and probably for that woman -- I always wanted to be extraordinary."

Whatever it was that his parents "hammered" into him gave him enough motivation to rise from poverty to prominence. He eventually cultivated an unwavering belief in himself.

It is often true that we don't let ourselves have more than we think we deserve. Not that any of us deserves more than anyone else, but perhaps most of us deserve more than we let ourselves have. If we feel trapped in a relationship which is destructive or unfulfilling, we deserve more. If we are employed in a job which under-utilizes our true abilities and skills, we deserve more. If we believe that life is going nowhere, we deserve more. Poitier was taught that he was *somebody* and, therefore, allowed himself to pursue what many believed to be unattainable goals.

You, too, are *somebody*. You are a person of infinite worth. Will you allow yourself to experience what you really deserve?

The Way Home

Steve Reinhard tells a heartwarming story about a little girl who walked home from school every day. The quickest way home for her was through the town's cemetery. It was her favorite time of day. She loved to feel the breeze in her hair and to watch the birds. Sometimes she just threw herself on the soft, green grass and watched the clouds turn into castles and angels and great white stallions. As she skipped around gravestones, she whistled her favorite tune or sang a song. Other times, she liked to kneel down and read the names and dates on gravestones and to glide her fingers across the engraved lettering. She particularly enjoyed those walks through the graveyard.

Still, her friends asked, "Why do you walk through the cemetery after school?"

"That's easy," she would always reply. "Because it's the way home."

In an ultimate sense, that is true, isn't it? The way home is always through the cemetery. And it does not have to be a fearful passage at all, this way that leads home. It is a trip we can actually look forward to with joy.

Which is good to know, especially when we're holding the hand of one who is about to make the voyage. Or when we are ready to go ourselves.

P.S.

Margaret Daniel's grave at Hollywood Cemetery, Richmond, Virginia, says this: "She always said her feet were killing her, but nobody believed her."

Reason to Smile

Comedian George Burns said that he was advised: "Let a smile be your umbrella." He said, "I tried that once. I had pneumonia for six weeks and shrunk a $450 suit."

All right. Maybe it won't keep you dry in the rain, but there are other good reasons to smile. Author Brian Tracy tells us that the face requires 12 muscles to smile and 103 to frown. (Who counts these things?) He also says that whenever you smile at another person, it puts them at ease and raises their self-esteem. And if that isn't enough, when you smile it releases endorphins in your brain and gives you a feeling of well-being and contentment.

So a smile benefits the giver as well as the receiver. It's like receiving a gift in return every time we give one away!

Rabbi Hirsch gives more reasons to smile:

★ Smiling is a universal language.
★ People will enjoy being around you when you smile.
★ Smiling reduces stress, which may improve your overall health.

★ Smiling will change the sound qualities of your voice when you speak or sing.

★ A smile costs nothing but gives much. It enriches those who receive it, without making poorer those who give.

★ It takes but a moment, but the memory of it lasts forever.

★ It cannot be bought, begged, borrowed, or stolen, for it is something that is of no value to anyone until it is given away.

★ And finally, some people are too tired to give you a smile. Give them one of yours, as no one needs a smile so much as one who has no more to give.

Why not give out a few extra smiles today -- just for the fun of it!

P.S.

Isn't it true? In seeking happiness for others you find it for yourself.

Squash Power

Do you know how strong you really are? In an interesting experiment at Amherst College (Massachusetts) a band of steel was secured around a young squash. As the squash grew, it exerted pressure on the steel band. Researchers wanted to know just how strong a squash could be, so they measured the force it brought to bear on its constraints. They initially estimated that it might be able to exert as much as 500 pounds of pressure.

In one month, the squash was pressing 500 pounds. In two months it was applying 1,500 pounds and, when it reached 2,000 pounds, researchers had to strengthen the steel band. The squash eventually brought 5,000 pounds of pressure to bear on the band -- when the rind split open.

They opened it up and found it to be inedible, as it was filled with tough, course fibers that had grown to push against the constraining obstacle. The plant required great amounts of nutrients to gain the strength needed to break its bonds, and its roots extended great distances in all directions. The squash had single-handedly taken over the garden space!

We have no idea just how strong we really

can be! If a squash can exert that much physical pressure, how much more strength can human beings apply to a situation? Most of us are stronger than we realize. I am told that it was Eleanor Roosevelt who observed, "A woman is like a tea bag; you never know how strong she is until she gets into hot water." (I suspect the same is true of men.)

Does an obstacle you are presently facing loom large before you? Does it seem just too big? Perhaps overwhelming? If so, remember the squash. Its single-minded purpose was to break the bonds which held it. If you patiently focus your energy -- what problem can stand against the great mental, spiritual and physical strength you can bring to bear?

Getting A Busy Signal

Two natural gas company service personnel, a senior training supervisor and a young trainee, were out checking meters in a suburban neighborhood. They parked their truck at the end of an alley and worked their way to the other end.

At the last house, a woman looking out her kitchen window watched the two men as they checked her gas meter. When they finished, the senior supervisor, proud of his physical condition, challenged his younger co-worker to a foot race back to their truck.

As they approached the truck, they realized that the woman was huffing and puffing right behind them. They stopped and asked her what was wrong.

Gasping for breath, she replied, "When I saw two gas men running as hard as you two were, I figured I'd better run, too!"

In another way, we spend a great deal of time running, don't we? We are running to catch up at work. We are running to keep up at home. We speak of "running" errands. We "rush" off, we drive in the "fast" lane, we stop at the "Quick" mart, we buy "fast" food, we use the "express" lane, and we "hurry" back so we can "race" through our meal. Too often our lives are lived in fast forward. No wonder we "run down"!

One telecommunications company executive went to see his doctor. She listened to her patient's heart, shook her head and said, "All I get is a busy signal."

An important part of reducing harmful stress is to simply slow down. Take a walk. Spend some time alone. Be still. Listen to your soul. Surprisingly, you may find you have *more* energy left for the important work. In time, you may wonder why you ever rushed at all.

P.S.

You know you are suffering from too much stress when you page yourself, because when it's set to vibrate, it's almost like getting a massage.

And Then Some

How wonderful it would be if there were a simple formula for success! "Follow these steps and you will be successful in business, as a parent, as a student, in your vocation or in any endeavor you attempt."

I think of the man who was honored as "Businessperson of the Year." At the presentation dinner, a newspaper reporter asked him, "To what do you owe your great success and prosperity?"

"Five things contributed to my success," said the man. "First, I always treated people fairly. Second, I always offered a fair price. Third, I was always honest. Fourth, I was always generous to my employees. And fifth, my Aunt Edna died a few years back and left me two and a half million dollars."

Certainly, the top four items on his list are well worth following, though they are no guarantee of success. For a variety of reasons, some of which are outside our control (like Aunt Edna), our lives are filled with successes and failures, all of which contribute to our growth. But some of the sagest advice I've heard on the subject of success comes from Professor Richard Weaver, who taught at

Bowling Green State University, Ohio. He says that what often sets a successful person apart from others are three simple words: "and then some."

Those people who tend to achieve what they want from life do what is expected of them -- and then some. They are thoughtful to others; they are considerate and kind -- and then some. They meet their obligations and responsibilities fairly -- and then some. They are good friends to their friends -- and then some. They can be counted on in an emergency -- and then some.

By going beyond the expectations of others, they demonstrate every day their desire to do their best and to be their best. They, too, fail and blunder, but in the end, they can be counted on to pick up the pieces and move forward.

Those are three words worth remembering. Count on them to help build a quality life -- and then some.

When Love Is For Real

Two lovers were talking and she said to him, "I don't have a lot of money. I don't have a brand new sports car and a yacht like Lisa Turner, but I love you with all my heart."

He said to her, "I love you, too. But tell me more about Lisa Turner." Tennessee Williams might have said that he had "all the sincerity of a bird-hunter's whistle."

If love is anything, I believe it must be genuine. It must be sincere.

That word "sincere" has some interesting roots. I'm told it comes from the ancient marble quarries of Rome. Apparently, unscrupulous stone dealers covered the marble's imperfections with wax. The practice eventually became illegal, as the Roman Empire certified that all marble must be "sine cera" or "sincerus," meaning without wax -- genuine. So, to be sincere is to be genuine. And love, at its best, is likewise "free of deceit," or genuine.

Genuine love is for real. And it's the stuff whole and happy lives are built on.

P.S.

Frederick L. Collins has said that there are two types of people: those who come into a room and say, "Well, here I am!" and those who come in and say, "Ah, there you are!"

When Suffering Visits

I recall sitting with a woman a few years ago whose only son had unexpectedly died. I had sat in the same place a couple of years before when her husband had passed away. Of course, the loss of her son was opening the wound, not yet fully healed, caused by her husband's death.

With tear-filled eyes and pursed lips she lamented, "Oh, how terrible life can be! Isn't this world a terrible place?"

What could I say? On the one hand, I believe that the world can be a wonderful and enchanting place. There are times of fun and joy and happiness. I even believe life can be an exciting adventure!

On the other hand, for her right then, the world was indeed a terrible place. All of her family was gone. She faced the prospect of countless days filled with heartache and endless nights of loneliness. Such grief cannot be dismissed with a quick, "Oh, it will be all right. You'll be fine." Or, "Don't worry, he's in a better place." Regardless of whether these statements are true, to minimize her feelings of loss at that moment would have done her a great disservice. More than anything, she needed some-one to understand her pain and confusion.

"It's a difficult world to live in," I finally said, taking her hand. "I'm sorry."

She eventually did get through both losses. It was difficult and took time, but with help from her friends and hope from her faith she was able put her life back together. She was able to laugh and sing again.

When the world seems like a terrible place, I think it is good to remember a few things:

★ Please don't blame yourself for something that may not be your fault. The death of a family member is a good example. There are some things which are beyond your control.

★ Remember that you *will* get through it, even if it doesn't seem so at the time. One widowed woman remarked to me six months after her spouse's death, "I used to have more bad days than good days. Now I have more good days!" She was moving through her loss.

★ Remember that you are not isolated. Please reach out to others when you hurt. And draw upon your spiritual resources. You are not alone.

This world can be fun and challenging, filled with laughter and happiness! But when suffering visits, remembering these things can help ease the hurt.

Simply Amazed!

I recall a story about Noah Webster (of dictionary fame), who suddenly found himself one day in an embarrassing situation. He was caught kissing the maid in the kitchen pantry by none other than his wife.

"Why Noah!" she exclaimed. "I'm surprised!"

Always the semanticist, Noah replied, "No, my dear, you're amazed. *I'm* surprised!"

No, I don't know how they ever resolved that situation. But I do know that surprise and amazement are important if we are to make the most of life's journey. People are dying to really love life. But they have, too often, forfeited the present in order to worry about the future or lament the past.

Ruth Carter Stapleton wrote a succinct philosophy of life in 1981, which was later read at her graveside service. She said: "Time is passing. Each day is a glorious opportunity to live and enjoy. Today I will let the past die -- all the undone things, all the misjudged things.... Today, there are new pleasures, new challenges, new magic."

If she allowed herself to be surprised by the present, could she help but be amazed every day by the "pleasures," "challenges" and "magic" all around her? And how about you? Are you ready to put aside concern for the past and future long enough to truly experience the present? Are you ready to be amazed?

P.S.

Living in the present isn't always easy. As one person said, "Just when I was getting used to yesterday, along came today."

When the Whole World Stinks

Do you remember the story of the sailor who over-imbibed and fell asleep at his table? His buddies smeared a bit of strong smelling cheese dip on his mustache, which caused him to wake up and look around. He sniffed and then walked outside, sniffed again and came back in, walked out and back in one more time and finally sat back down in his seat. "It's no use," he said to his friend, "the whole world stinks!"

Ever felt that way? We have all experienced bad days and horrible situations. We've felt trapped, helpless and, at times, hopeless. We may have even believed that the whole world stinks.

But I like the tremendous way one woman has learned to approach living. She grew up in extreme poverty, but was privileged to be in a Sunday School class taught by a young woman named Alice Freeman Palmer, who was later to become president of Wellesley College. One Sunday, the teacher asked the children to find something beautiful in their homes, and then tell the other children about it the next week.

The following Sunday, when the little girl was asked what she found that was beautiful at home, she thought of her impoverished condition and replied, "Nothing. There's nothing beautiful where I live, except...except the sunshine on our baby's curls."

Years later, long after Mrs. Palmer's untimely death, her husband was lecturing at a university in the western United States. He was approached by a distinguished looking woman who fondly recalled that she had been a member of his wife's Sunday School class. "I can remember that your wife once asked us to find something beautiful in our homes, and that I came back saying the only beautiful thing I could find was the sunshine on my sister's curls. But that assignment your wife made was the turning point in my life. I began to look for something beautiful wherever I was, and I've been doing it ever since." That one suggestion turned her life around.

If you have been thinking your "whole world stinks," the daily habit of looking for something beautiful can help you see the good that is in the world, and transform your hope into enough positive energy to build a life that counts.

Affirmation for Today

Ralph Waldo Emerson has accurately said, "One of the illusions of life is that the present hour is not the critical, decisive hour. Write it on your heart that every day is the best day of the year."

Today is an important day. That problem you solve, that decision you make, that time you enjoy can shape your whole life. The way you and I approach today, and each day, is crucial. Our lives are built by a series of days like today.

I discovered an affirmation that can help in living each day fully:

Today I will live through the next 24 hours and not try to tackle all of life's problems at once.

Today I will improve myself, body, mind and spirit.

Today I will refuse to spend time worrying about what might happen if...

Today I will not imagine what I would do if things were different. They are not different. I will do my best with what material I have.

Today I will find the grace to let go of resentments of others and self-condemnation over past mistakes.

Today I will not try to change, or improve, anybody but me.

Today I will act toward others as though this will be my last day on earth.

Today I will be unafraid. I will enjoy what is beautiful, and I will believe that as I give to the world, the world will give to me.

Whether these are the best of times or the worst of times, these are the only times we've got. Live each day fully and you will look back on a life that made a difference.

Thermometers and Thermostats

Do you know the difference between a thermometer and a thermostat? A thermometer simply measures the temperature. It doesn't do anything about it.

A thermostat measures the temperature and then responds. If the temperature is too high, a thermostat may shut off the heat. If the temperature is too low, a thermostat may trigger heat to turn on. It measures temperature and it does something about it.

While a thermometer is a passive tool, a thermostat is an active tool. They both experience the temperature, but a thermostat responds.

Some people are like thermometers -- they passively allow what may harm them to just happen. They have problems and difficulties and they believe there isn't anything that can be done about it. They feel helpless as they watch life happen. They feel as if they have no power.

Others are more like thermostats. When they are faced with difficulty, they kick into action. They believe that something can be done; a solution can be found; a hurt can be healed. They respond; they make decisions; they go into motion.

Advice columnist Ann Landers said, "If I were asked to give what I consider the single most useful bit of advice for all humanity, it would be this: Expect trouble as an inevitable part of life. When it comes, hold your head high, look it squarely in the eye, and say, 'I will be bigger than you. You cannot defeat me.'" In other words, respond courageously and creatively.

Do you know that you can be bigger than any trouble that comes your way? If you have become stuck because you feel frightened or helpless, it is time to respond. It is time to go into motion. It is time to activate your faith. When you become bigger than your problem, it cannot defeat you.

Today -- will you be a thermometer or a thermostat?

P.S.

Don't take life too seriously. It's not permanent.

A Touching Moment

Are you meeting a friend for lunch? According to *The Farmer's Almanac*, if you are American you will probably touch each other twice an hour. If you are English, you may not touch each other at all. If you are French, you might touch each other 110 times an hour, and if you are Puerto Rican, you just might touch each other 180 times an hour.

There are obvious cultural differences in communication styles, but studies agree that touching is important to human development. Psychologist Wayne Dennis observed a group of babies in an orphanage where they were given practically no stimulation, including touch (Robert Ornstein and Paul Ehrlich, *New Mind*; New York, New York: A Touchstone Book, 1990). Most laid on their backs all day in bare cribs placed in bare rooms. They were touched only when their diapers were changed. At the end of one year, the children's development was about that of a six-month-old. The good news is that, once adopted into nurturing environments, these children quickly caught up to other children their age.

Human touch is vital. With it, we thrive. Without it, we wither. And it is good preventive medicine. It is simpler to hold a hand than to hold a consultation. A hanging head needs a shoulder under it. A back rub can be the easiest way to get a "monkey off someone's back." And the best way to get somebody's chin up is by lifting it with a gentle hand.

One of the best gifts you can give another may be an encouraging touch. And would you really mind if the gift were returned?

When Love Gives Out

A certain amount of conflict is a part of life. But conflict and violence are quite different.

One man tells about living next door to a bully. Last month the neighbor came up to him with hand extended. As he reached to shake hands, his neighbor grabbed him forcefully and threw him over his shoulder. "That's Judo," he said. "Picked it up in Japan."

The man went into his garage, came back out and cracked the bully over the head. "That's crowbar," he said. "Picked it up at Sears."

Some conflict is necessary, and many of us will wisely learn how to make conflicts with others both constructive and healthy. We will do well not to avoid daily conflict, but to resolve it quickly. And, of course, that doesn't mean to grab the crowbar, either.

Actually, I understand that the Chinese have a good idea, illustrated by a true story.

Two natives of Hong Kong were arguing loudly in the street. An American, who observed the altercation but could not speak the language, asked an Asian friend what they were arguing about.

"They are having a discussion about the ownership of a boat," came the reply.

"They're getting so wrought up, won't they start fighting soon?" the tourist asked.

"No," his friend said. "These men will not start fighting because each one knows the man who strikes the first blow admits his ideas just gave out."

It's true. Those individuals and societies who are quick to violence admit their ideas just gave out. As well as their love. For I must admit, if I strike the first blow, my love has given out. But when I approach that conflict with a head full of ideas and a heart full of love, I am astounded at how quickly things get settled!

A Matter of Trust

During a flight between New York and Chicago, the captain made this announcement over the plane's intercom: "Our number four engine has just been shut off because of mechanical trouble. There is nothing to worry about, however, and we can still finish the flight with just three engines. Besides, you will be reassured to know that we have four bishops on board."

An 86-year-old woman called the flight attendant and said, "Would you please tell the captain that I would rather have four engines and three bishops!" Experience taught her to place her trust in the aircraft rather than passengers -- even if they're bishops!

Experience, likewise, has taught us to be careful of what and whom we trust. We learn to be careful trusting risky investments, offers to make easy money, people we don't know, and anything that seems "too good to be true." We are sometimes even afraid to trust ourselves!

Helen Keller learned a great deal about trust in her life as one who was both sightless and deaf. She learned to trust people, upon whom she was often dependent. She learned to trust herself and lived a highly productive life in spite of her handicapping conditions. As a noted writer and thinker, she taught us that trust is vital to any happy life.

That great woman believed there are four great things to learn in life. They are:

★ To think clearly without hurry or confusion;
★ To love everyone sincerely;
★ To act in everything with the highest motives;
★ To trust God unhesitatingly.

Trust. It is a small word which can make a big difference.

P.S.

Speaking of trust, someone asked, "Should you trust a stockbroker who's married to a travel agent?"

Never Too Late

Standing at a busy Los Angeles intersection, I once noticed an interesting sight -- a shirtless old man in shorts and jogging shoes running toward me. He was in his seventies, short, with a huge barrel chest. His shoulders were wide and his stomach flat and hard. The skin on his thin arms and legs hung loose. His body glistened with sweat -- he had the appearance of an absolutely committed runner. When he approached the intersection, he continued to jog in place as he waited for the light to change.

I asked him, "Have you been running long?"

He said between breaths, "Today, four hours and twenty minutes."

Wow! *Four hours and twenty minutes of running! At his age!* He continued, his feet still pounding the concrete, "Some days I run 22 miles. Some days 12 miles."

I asked, "Do you race?"

"Three or four times a year." Maybe he figured he will taper off when he gets old.

I respect his commitment and focus. Because of a total dedication to the sport, he was an excellent runner. And he is living proof that it is never too late to pursue a passion!

Don't we all need something to get excited about? What if we were as focused in our enthusiasm and dedication? What could we do or become if we were as committed to those things we feel are important as he was to running?

You may build your body, but will you also build your mind? You may improve your social standing, but will you also improve your society? You may grow your bank account, but will you also grow your faith? You may build your business, but will you also build your character? You may heal a broken bone, but will you also heal a broken home? You may leave a will to your children, but will you also leave them a legacy?

It's never too late to pursue your passion.

Before Blasting Off

Lorraine Hansberry wrote a play called, "A Raisin in the Sun." In that play a sister is completely out of patience with her brother. He has been so disgusting in her eyes that she never again wants anything to do with him.

But her mother is wise. She tells her daughter that the time to love somebody is not when they have done well and made things easy for everyone. The time to love somebody is when "he's at his lowest and can't believe in himself 'cause the world done whipped him so."

She is telling her daughter that there is a time to patiently bear with another. And especially when that other is hard to love and angry because "the world done whipped him so."

Patiently bearing with another is not the same as allowing yourself to be abused. There is certainly a time to say, "No," especially when someone's behavior is destructive. But there is also a time for understanding and patience. It has been said that patience is the ability to count down before blasting off. And an old Chinese proverb has it that if you continually grind a bar of iron, you can make a needle of it. All it takes is patience.

If there is a time to call it quits, is there also a time for patient understanding? Is there someone who may need you to bear with them a little longer?

Friendly Fire

"Friendly fire," or fratricide, is a military term used when troops of one nation accidentally kill their own. Fratricide has tragically become a battlefield fact of life. David Foster in *Light and Life* (July 2, 1994), tells us George Washington reported that during the French and Indian War, 400 casualties resulted from soldiers who panicked and sent volley after volley into their own ranks.

Stonewall Jackson, Confederate general during the American Civil War, was killed in 1863 by his own soldiers as he galloped back into southern lines.

Perhaps 10% of American casualties of World War II and 15% to 20% during the Vietnam Conflict were the result of fratricide -- bombs which were dropped by accident; errant rifle fire; artillery shells landing on the wrong targets.

"Friendly fire" is the cause of countless casualties even today. Not in battle, but in the workplace and on the home front. Teachers who are assailed by parents "burn out" in just a few short years. In-fighting within groups brings down worthwhile organizations. Those in the helping professions are set upon by those they try to care for. Co-workers undermine one another, at the expense of productivity and emotional health. Spouses fire verbal (and sometimes physical) shots at one another until mortally wounded marriages finally die. Families fight amongst themselves with little regard for the damage wrought.

The loss from domestic "friendly fire" cannot be estimated. Yet these casualties are unnecessary and wasteful.

Someone said so well:

> *To come together is a beginning;*
> *To stay together is progress;*
> *To finish together is success.*

Can an organization or family succeed when it sustains damages from within? The solution to the problem of loss by friendly fire is found in the word "together." We have come together for important reasons. We are in it together. Through conflict and disagreement, we must stand together. And in the end, if we finish at all, we will finish together.

P.S.

There is another way to unity. Carl Zwanzig says, "Duct tape is like the Force. It has a light side, a dark side, and it holds the universe together...."

How Big Is Your Frying Pan?

Are you setting your sights too low?

I heard of a woman who fished all morning and never caught anything. But a man in the next boat was reeling in a fish every time she glanced over. Then, to make matters worse, he kept the small ones and threw the large ones back into the water!

She couldn't stand it any longer. She called over to him, "How come you're throwing the big ones back?"

He answered by holding up a little frying pan.

We may think that is silly but, in our minds, don't we all hold up frying pans? Every time we throw away a big idea, a magnificent dream or an exciting possibility, are we measuring it against a small frying pan?

We talk about making more money or becoming more successful, but I believe that this concept works in other, and sometimes more important, areas as well. We can *love* more than we ever dreamed possible! We can be *happier* and *live more fully* than we ever thought we could! What we can do or become is limited more by the size of the frying pan in our minds than by actual circumstances.

Author Brian Tracy reminds us that "you are not what you think you are, but what you think, you are." Think big. Dream big. Pray big...and look for big results. It all begins with changing the size of your thinking.

What would happen if you threw away the frying pan you have been using to measure the size of your dreams, and replaced it with a larger one? What would happen if you decided that it may really *be* possible to have a better relationship with the one you love, or that you actually *can* be happier and more fulfilled than you are now? What would happen if you decided never to settle for anything less than what you truly want? What if, from now on, you threw the *little* fish back and kept the *big* ones?

And what if you decided to begin today?

Wealth of Wisdom

One man said, "I had a brain scan and was told not to worry -- there was nothing there!" Which is all right because some of my best ideas over the years have come from others, anyway. And I have discovered that wisdom can be found in most any place and from most any person -- even the youngest of us.

It was a child who passed on this morsel: "If your sister hits you, don't hit her back. They always catch the second person." It is wisdom borne of hard experience.

Yet another child teaches us that "the best place to be when you are sad is in Grandma's lap."

Adults, too, have wisdom to share. One parent observed that "the best way to keep kids at home is to make the home a pleasant place to be... and let the air out of their car tires."

Wisdom can also be found among the youngest of us. And it will be shared by the most elderly too, if we listen. I am related by marriage to a woman who is 103 years old. During her 100th year, "Aunt Pearl" was asked to speak to a group of high school students. She offered a century of wisdom in a few short sentences: "Enrich your life by becoming a better person, a better student and an individual worthy of trust and faithful in your commitments. Aspire to help and not hinder in all your good and worthy undertakings. Use these words often: 'thank you,' 'please,' 'I'm sorry.' After living 100 years, I admonish you to think deeply, speak gently, work hard, give freely, pay promptly, pray earnestly and be kind."

Wisdom doesn't come much better than that.

P.S.

More wisdom from kids. Bart, age 9, was asked how to make someone fall in love with you. He suggests, "One way is to take the girl out to eat. Make sure it's something she likes to eat. French fries usually work for me."

Trouble Box

They call it a "trouble box." It is a brightly colored, egg-sized box found among natives of Guatemala. Inside are placed six tiny dolls. Families often keep one inside their homes. When trouble befalls a family member, the disturbed person takes out one of the tiny dolls and talks the problem over with it. Then the doll is set aside and the problem forgotten.

If another difficulty comes up that same day, another doll is selected to "listen." Each doll is then set aside to mull over the situation. Finally, at the end of every day, the dolls are gathered and replaced in the box, ready for tomorrow.

The idea sounds intriguing! One doll for one problem. And it makes psychological sense. Many of our troubles cannot be acted upon immediately and just become a source of destructive worry. But if we can sufficiently talk through a problem and then, if no action is required, set it aside, we can go about the business of living unencumbered.

The formula is simple: a) talk through the problem, either with a caring friend or by yourself; b) if it requires action, do what must be done; and c) if no action is called for, then set it aside and focus your energies in more productive areas. Talk. Act. Move on.

Remember, worry is not the same as healthy concern. Worry is like a rocking chair -- it gives you something to do, but gets you nowhere. Decide to worry less, and you may find yourself living more!

The Richest Person in the World

I will always remember Stella. Elderly, blind and living alone, one might think she should have spun long tales of hardship and misery. And I suppose she could have told such stories, but she made little room in her life for self-pity. She might have mentioned the deaths of friends and family, including her husband; the glaucoma which finally claimed her eyesight; the small pension on which she was forced to subsist and the arthritis which kept her homebound in a little trailer house. And nobody could blame her had she despaired that she had grown so dependent on others.

She never did lament about all her hardships, either past or present. But I frequently recall her enumerating her good fortune. Speaking of her son, she often said: "My Jimmy came to see me today. He's so good to me!" Of her friends, she often commented: "I've been talking on the phone all morning. I'm so thankful I have such good friends." Then, with a slap on her knee and a broad smile on her lips, she would invariably exclaim, "I'm the richest person in the world!"

And maybe she was! She had love. She found it in her friends, her family and her faith. She had everything she needed for a happy and fulfilled life. And what's more, she knew it.

Stella spoke of her upcoming 90th birthday. "All my family will be here," she smiled. And with that familiar slap on her knee, she exclaimed, "You know, I'm the richest person in the world!"

But she barely made that birthday celebration herself. Several days prior she was laid in a hospital bed and slipped into a coma. Her family was told she would die shortly. I felt sad that she would not experience her long-awaited celebration.

However, a strange thing happened. On the day of her birthday, she opened her eyes and greeted the smiling faces of family and friends surrounding her bed. She sat up and enjoyed birthday cake while someone read cards. They told her they loved her and they said, "Good-bye." At one point, she looked at me with that familiar twinkle in her eye, smiled and whispered, "I'm the richest person in the world!"

Stella went to sleep that night and slipped peacefully away. I have often wondered if she felt sorry for those who have everything but happiness. After all, they could be just as wealthy and happy as she, if they only realized that the greatest of all riches is love.

Thanks to Stella, I have now decided to become the richest person in the world! And I think I can!

P.S.

Virginia Satir (1916-1988), psychotherapist and author, has said, "I believe the greatest gift I can conceive of having from anyone is to be seen by them, heard by them, to be understood and touched by them."

In Focus

In reading a mortality chart, I discovered something truly amazing. A great number of people die each year from a disease I had never heard of! Of course, there was the predictable number who died of heart attacks, cancer, stroke, accidents and the like, but at the bottom of the chart was one which surprised me. It was called "miscellaneous." Apparently, a large number of people die of "miscellaneous" every year!

I think I understand why. I suffer from "miscellaneous" when I go in too many directions at once. When I am directionless and scattered, the disease begins to take over. Soon my self-esteem is affected and I feel as if I'm doing nothing important. Flitting here and there, I have no overriding purpose and I feel as if my life is spinning out of control. It must be a terrible way to die!

However, I believe there is a cure for the disease. It's called "focus." A focused person is one who knows what is important and follows the path. She may have many interests, but one calling. A focused person hears one voice more clearly than the others...and follows. Some call it pursuing a mission. Some call it knowing your purpose. Others call it being centered. Whatever it is called, a focused life can be meaningful and happy.

Not every path should be followed, and not every goal should become a life's calling. But a truly worthy focus can raise a life from mediocrity and save it from a slow death by miscellaneous.

Are you in focus?

An Incredible Feeling

Newscaster Paul Harvey once told about a woman who called the Butterball Turkey Company and said that she had a turkey which had been in her freezer for 23 years. She asked if it was still any good. She was told that if her freezer was at least zero degrees, then it was probably safe enough to eat. But they wouldn't recommend that she eat it. The flavor would have deteriorated considerably. She said, "That's what we thought. I guess we'll just give it to the church."

Some people give off the top. Others scrape it off the bottom! But people who enjoy giving the most, give straight from their hearts.

Santa Claus is becoming a universal symbol of giving. Millions of children write letters to Santa each year, in hopes that they won't be forgotten during his annual giving spree. Did you know that the U.S. Post Office is actually finding ways to answer all of those letters to Santa Claus? They used to just stick them in the dead letter box. But now some cities have programs that allow people to sort through those letters and become "Santas" to others in need.

One letter, which might have been discarded a few years ago, was from a boy named Donny who wrote that he wanted a bike for Christmas and "some food and what I really need is love."

Another letter, from a young mother, said, "I lost my job...and I cannot afford to give my two children the things they need for the winter months."

In some cities now, anyone can help by going through the piles of Santa's mail held at their local post office. They choose a letter and respond however they can. Anyone can be Santa!

"I like to go to their home on Christmas Eve," one generous Santa said. One year he bought presents for four children and a ham for their mother. "The feeling you get is just incredible."

That incredible feeling can only come one way -- when we give from the heart. This is a truth which is not limited to a particular holiday season or tradition. Whether we give food, an hour of time or a hug, when we give from the heart we give our best.

But let me offer a word of caution. If you choose to give from the heart, be careful. You might just be overwhelmed by the most incredible feeling! And if you continue in this behavior, the feeling may become permanent!

P.S.

Someone has beautifully said, "Go confidently in the direction of your dreams! Live the life you've imagined."

A Miracle Morning

In her poem "Aurora Leigh," Elizabeth Barrett Browning wrote:

Earth's crammed with heaven,
And every common bush afire with God;
But only he who sees, takes off his shoes,
The rest sit round it and pluck blackberries.

I have certainly plucked my share of blackberries, blind to what wonder there is in life. But on occasion I have also had my eyes opened by others, a bit more sensitive and aware. I cherish those moments and recall them when life gets too routine and ordinary. One such incident occurred many years ago.

I stumbled out the door of a mountain cabin where I was spending the weekend working with youth and their families at a rustic retreat center. I had a 6:30 a.m. appointment to keep and squinted from the early autumn sun peeking over pine-blanketed mountaintops.

"Today is a miracle!" spoke a young, enthusiastic voice behind me. I turned toward the radiant face of my teen-aged friend.

"How?" I asked her. I wasn't sure if I could handle any excitement this early in the morning.

"Think about it," she smiled. "The sun rose, didn't it?"

"Yeah." I found it easy to hide any enthusiasm. It seemed to rise on every other morning without any help from me.

"That's a miracle! It is miraculous that the earth turns as it does. At night, the sun goes down and in the morning it rises. It just happens!"

I pretty much had this figured out years ago, I thought, as I rubbed sleep from my eyes. I was also busy thinking about how to get a cup of coffee.

"And look at the mountains! Covered with trees and grass, they look so beautiful. And there," she pointed, "a valley. It's all a miracle!"

"What have I stumbled into?" I thought. "And *where* is the coffee?"

"Wildflowers blooming," she continued. "It all smells so fresh and clean and so good." She took a deep breath. Her blue eyes sparkled. "All of nature receives water and light. Things grow and blossom -- it is all so beautiful." Maybe it wasn't coffee I needed...but whatever she had gotten into!

I didn't know if it was her bubbly personality or the freshness of the morning, but I began to sense her enchantment with the daybreak. A little, anyway. Somehow, she had me believing that the day did hold a certain magic.

Then, with a smile which seemed to make her blonde curls laugh, she gave her pronouncement a note of finality. "And best of all, it will happen again tomorrow. And the next day! And the next!" She sighed. "It's a miracle morning!"

My young friend showed wisdom beyond her years. For her, earth was "crammed with heaven" and "every bush afire." She should never want for happiness, for she had already learned, at such an early age, to find wonder in the commonplace and to feel gratitude for the ordinary. If each day for her is a miracle, then a lifetime will be no less than a marvelous extravaganza!

Is EVERYTHING Going Wrong?

A humorous story tells about a speeding motorist who was caught by radar from a police helicopter in the sky. An officer pulled him over and began to issue a traffic ticket. "How did you know I was speeding?" the frustrated driver asked.

The police officer pointed somberly toward the sky. "You mean," asked the motorist, "that even He is against me?"

It's like the man who said, "It feels like the whole world is against me...but I know that's not true. Some of the smaller countries are neutral."

When we have a problem, it can often feel as if everything in our life is going wrong. We may tend to think that *everybody* is upset, that *nobody* cares or that *everything* is falling apart.

To think more clearly and to solve your problems more effectively, try letting go of these destructive beliefs:

★ Let go of the idea that your problem is permanent. Few troubles last forever. And those that cannot be solved can usually be managed.

★ Let go of the idea that your problem is pervasive. Few problems affect every area of your life.

★ Let go of the idea that your problem is personal. There is nothing wrong with you because you have a problem. All capable, lovable and successful people have plenty of problems.

Remember, worms cannot fall down. But human beings can -- and will. Let go of these destructive beliefs and you may be amazed at how much better you feel already!

P.S.

Speaking of troubles...someone said, "Life is like an ice cream cone...just when you think you've got it licked, it drips on you."

A Work of Art

Edward Fischer writes in *Notre Dame Magazine* (February, 1983), that a leper (or, more correctly, a sufferer of Hanson's Disease) in Fiji followed the leading of his twisted hands. He became an internationally known artist. "My sickness I see as a gift of God leading me to my life's work," he said. "If it had not been for my sickness, none of these things would have happened."

As a young girl, Jessamyn West had tuberculosis. She was so sick that she was sent away to die. During that time she developed her skill as a writer and authored numerous novels in her lifetime.

That great author Flannery O'Connor suffered numerous ailments -- lupus struck her at 25 and she walked only with the aid of crutches for the final fourteen years of her life. She noted, however, that this illness narrowed her activities in such a way that she had time for the real work of her life, which was writing.

Some people succeed in spite of handicaps. Others succeed because of them. The truth is, our problems help to make us what we are. Those who suffer often learn the value of compassion. Those who struggle often learn perseverance. And those who fall down often teach others how to rise again. Our troubles can shape us in ways a carefree existence cannot.

A story is told of an Eastern village which, through the centuries, was known for its exquisite pottery. Especially striking were its urns; high as tables, wide as chairs, they were admired around the globe for their strong form and delicate beauty.

Legend has it that when each urn was apparently finished, there was one final step. The artist broke it -- and then put it back together with gold filigree.

An ordinary urn was then transformed into a priceless work of art. What seemed finished wasn't, until it was broken.

So it is with people! Broken by hardships, disappointments and tragedy, they can become disappointed and bitter. But when mended by a hand of infinite patience and love, the finished product will be a work of exquisite beauty and effectiveness; a life which could only reach its wholeness after it was broken.

If you feel broken, remember that you are a work of art! And you may not actually be complete until the pieces are reassembled and bonded with a golden filigree of love.

Keeping Up with Yesterday?

James Myers in *A Treasury of Military Humor* (Springfield, Illinois: The Lincoln-Herndon Press, Inc., 1990), tells an all-too-true story which comes from the American Civil War. General Stonewall Jackson recruited a man named Miles, who had a reputation as a superb bridge builder. Because bridges were needed to be built or rebuilt quickly, Miles became a valuable asset to the army.

One day, retreating Union troops set fire to a bridge and Jackson called upon Miles to get his men ready to prepare a foundation for a new bridge. He told him that the engineers would have plans ready in record time.

The next day, Jackson called for Miles and asked him if the engineers had given him their plans yet. "General," Miles drawled, "we done got the foundation built but I cain't tell ya whether them pictures is done or not."

There is a time for careful planning, it's true. But there is also a time for quick and decisive action. Miles seemed to know that the urgency of the situation required him to just do what needed to be done.

Our greatest obstacle to "doing what needs to be done" is not careful planning. Though many of us have admirable plans and worthy resolutions, we often simply never get around to doing what we have determined to do! We procrastinate. And unfortunately, we often miss an opportunity to do something decisive today, for as Don Marquis has said, "Procrastination is the art of keeping up with yesterday."

Or maybe you have been thinking that you would like to procrastinate less, but just haven't gotten around to it yet. If so, perhaps these words will help:

He was going to be all that a mortal could be...
tomorrow.
None should be stronger or braver than he...
tomorrow.
A friend who was troubled and weary he knew,
Who'd be glad of a lift and who needed it, too,
On him he would call to see
what he could do...tomorrow.

Each morning he'd stack up the letters he'd
write...tomorrow.
And he thought of the friends he would fill with de-
light...tomorrow.
It was too bad indeed; he was busy each day,
And hadn't a minute to stop on his way;
"More time I'll give to others," he'd say...
"tomorrow."

The greatest of workers this man would have
been...tomorrow.
The world would have known him, had he ever
seen...tomorrow.
But the fact is he died, and faded from view,
And all that he left here when living was through
Was a mountain of things he intended to do...
tomorrow.

If there is a time and a season for everything, then is today the day to do that thing you have been putting off?

P.S.

The Top Ten Reasons Not to Procrastinate:
1.

Beautiful Old People

A 104-year-young woman was being interviewed by a reporter. "And what do you think is the best thing about 104?" the journalist asked.

"No peer pressure," she replied.

When I was in college, I worked in an after school daycare center with a marvelous woman in her mid-seventies. One day she was complaining about her age. "All my friends are old and crippled," she remarked. "They're either crippled in their legs or crippled in their minds."

I know that growing older is not easy, at any age. Columnist Dave Barry talked about it when he turned 40. "If I don't warm up before throwing a football," he said, "I have to wait approximately until the next presidential administration before I attempt to do this again."

But even with its aches and pains and a variety of other problems, aging does have an upside. Sister Mary Gemma Brunke has so beautifully written:

"It is the old apple trees that are decked with the loveliest blossoms. It is the ancient redwoods that rise to majestic heights. It is the old violins that produce the richest tones. It is the aged wine that tastes the sweetest. It is ancient coins, stamps and furniture that people seek. It is the old friends that are loved the best. Thank God for the blessings of age and the wisdom, patience and maturity that go with it. Old is wonderful!"

"Beautiful people are acts of nature," it has been said, "but beautiful old people are works of art."

I hope someday to be a work of art.

All the Advice You'll Ever Need

A popular T-shirt reads, "Upon the Advice of My Attorney, My Shirt Bears No Message at This Time." Perhaps the counsel of others is occasionally heeded, but I know that advice is not something people crave. Which is why it is sometimes said that free advice is worth about as much as you pay for it. Or put another way: "Plain advice is free. The right answer will cost plenty."

Our penchant for not wanting advice holds true across the generations. President Harry Truman once said, "I have found the best way to give advice to your children is to find out what they want and then advise them to do it."

Nor is our aversion to advice just a peculiar sign of the times. As one boy wrote in an essay on the ancient Greek philosopher Socrates: "Socrates was a man who went around town giving his advice and opinions, so...they poisoned him!" What this student lacks in historical accuracy he more than makes up for in his sense about how well most advice is received.

Not all advice should be discarded, however. Nor should we overlook wisdom from unlikely sources. Like the "uneducated." And the aged.

I have a faded letter clipped from a newspaper many years ago. The author published some counsel given him by his grandmother who had died some 60 years prior, and who had never attended school. She offered it printed on a slip of paper, accompanied by the words, "All the advice you'll ever need to have a good life." I find it worth remembering. Here is what she wrote:

"Wash what is dirty. Water what is dry. Heal what is wounded. Warm what is cold. Guide what goes off the road. Love people who are least lovable, because they need it most."

Enough days spent refreshing, healing, warming, guiding and loving will add up to a good life, significant and well-lived.

P.S.

Speaking of advice, one person says, "Always remember you're unique, just like everyone else."

Getting the Anger Out

I learned that a woman in Arkansas called her local police department. She asked about the penalty for fighting. The sergeant told her that she could be charged with assault and battery. The fine was $100.

"Oh, I want to beat up my sister," she said, "and I wanted to see if I can afford it."

Anger must certainly be expressed, but this woman discovered that there is a price for expressing it inappropriately. Which is why, in the Japanese town of Yamanakako, visitors will pay hefty sums simply for the chance to vent their anger in Yoshie Ogasawara's "Relief Room," the main attraction of her four-story fun house. There, stressed-out business persons, jilted lovers and enraged spouses can smash a large porcelain vase, hurl ceramic ware into a soapstone peach tree from China and break a few ceramic clowns in an attempt to express their pent-up rage. The relief room owes its phenomenal success to our human need to express anger appropriately.

But still the most effective way of dealing with anger is to express it in words. "Talk it out" with the person with whom you are upset. As William Blake wrote:

I was angry with my friend,
I told my wrath, my wrath did end.
I was angry with my foe.
I told it not, my wrath did grow.

Anger must be "told" to be stilled. And if it is not possible to talk directly with the offending person, find a good listener. Sometimes, just "getting it out" is enough.

Further, talk it out soon, since unacknowledged anger is a malignant tumor. "Don't let the sun set on your anger," but rather strive to finally let go of each day's resentment in order to keep a clean slate.

Talking is still the best way to work through life's issues. And besides, this way you get to keep the dishes for company!

Gift of Peace

In the midst of a world at war, Eleanor Roosevelt captured the mood at Christmas 1942. "How completely the character of Christmas has changed this year," she wrote in her newspaper column. "I could no more say to you a 'Merry Christmas' without feeling a catch in my throat than I could fly to the moon!"

In September 1945, Navy chief radioman Walter G. Germann wrote his son from a ship anchored in Tokyo Bay to tell him that the formal surrender of Japan would soon be signed. "When you get a little older you may think war to be a great adventure -- take it from me, it's the most horrible thing ever done by (humans)," he wrote. "I'll be home this Christmas...." Home. To a world at peace.

In 1955 a thirteen-year-old Japanese girl died of "the atom bomb disease" -- radiation-induced leukemia. Sadako was one of many who suffered the after-effects of the bombs dropped on Hiroshima and Nagasaki in 1945.

Japanese myth has it that cranes live for a thousand years, and anyone who folds 1000 paper cranes will have a wish granted. So during her illness, Sadako folded paper cranes, and with each crane she wished that she would recover from her illness. She folded 644 cranes before she left this life, and this world, behind.

Sadako's classmates, however, folded 356 more cranes so that she could be buried with a thousand paper cranes. Friends collected money from children all over Japan to erect a monument to Sadako in Hiroshima's Peace Park. The inscription reads:

This is our cry,
This is our prayer,
Peace in the world.

Each year people place paper cranes at the base of the statue to recall the tragedy of war and to celebrate humanity's undying hope for peace. In some places around the world, people fold paper cranes each holiday season to use as decorations and as a symbol of their deep desire for lasting peace.

However you celebrate your holiday seasons, is there a better time than the present to recommit our world to a lasting peace? Let war become a fact of the past as we join our hearts in union with one another. Fold a crane. Light a candle. Say a prayer.

May we decide now and forevermore to seek the peaceful solution, the loving response. May it begin at home. This may be, by far, the best gift our generation can give the world.

P.S.

One newspaper editor stated the obvious... "War Dims Hope for Peace." Other actual headlines which state the obvious are, "If Strike Isn't Settled Quickly, It May Last a While," and "Cold Wave Linked to Temperatures." (I no longer read the papers as much as I used to....)

Pay Attention!

A funny story circulated recently about Sir Arthur Conan Doyle, creator of the fictional detective Sherlock Holmes. Doyle evidently told of a time when he climbed into a taxicab in Paris. Before he could utter a word, the driver turned to him and asked, "Where can I take you, Mr. Doyle?"

Doyle was flabbergasted. He asked the driver if he had ever seen him before.

"No, sir," the driver responded, "I have never seen you before." Then he explained: "This morning's paper had a story about you being on vacation in Marseilles. This is the taxi stand where people who return from Marseilles always arrive. Your skin color tells me you have been on vacation. The ink spot on your right index finger suggests to me that you are a writer. Your clothing is very English, and not French. Adding up all those pieces of information, I deduced that you are Sir Arthur Conan Doyle."

"This is truly amazing!" the writer exclaimed. "You are a real-life counterpart to my fictional creation, Sherlock Holmes!"

"There is one other thing," the driver said. "What is that?"

"Your name is on the front of your suitcase."

Perhaps the driver was no master detective, but he *was* observant! He paid attention, and paying attention is an important part of living fully.

"Life isn't a matter of milestones, but of moments," Rose Fitzgerald Kennedy aptly said. A life lived to the full is lived from moment to moment, rather than from milestone to milestone. It is more of a series of days in which we truly pay attention, than a few major events along the way.

Speaker Alan Loy McGinnis tells of a New York City sculptor named Louise. She made her home in one of the most dilapidated neighborhoods of the city. But, by paying attention to her surroundings, she found endless beauty and inspiration. She marveled at the elegance in the varying patterns of the sun and the moon reflected on tenement windows. In an object as ordinary as a chair she could see something extraordinary. "The chair isn't so hot," she once pointed out, "but look at its shadow." By paying attention, she was able to see what others might miss.

Pay attention! To the things of life. To people. To events. To your senses. Even to the ordinary. Pay attention to the moments and your life will never lack beauty and splendor. By making the most of the moments, you make the most of the years.

Adjust Your Sails

You remember the story about the woman who shook her son awake in the morning. "Get up and get ready for school," she urged. "You're going to be late!"

"Ah, Mom," he pleaded, "I don't want to go to school. The kids don't like me; the teachers are against me; even the custodian hates me. Give me three good reasons to go."

"All right," she agreed. "It's 6:30. You're 45 years old. And you're the principal!"

Every day we climb from bed, we decide how to face the day. Will we dread it or will we anticipate it? Will we resist it or will we welcome it?

Few persons have made us as aware of the power of our attitudes as the late Dr. Norman Vincent Peale. In his book *In God We Trust* (Nashville: Thomas Nelson Publishers, 1994), he tells about a woman he describes as "a nice lady," but "she got all tired out by eight o'clock in the morning. And she wasn't even out of her bed by then," he said. The problem was that she "lay there thinking of all the terrible things that were going to happen to her, how badly everything would turn out, how many problems she had, how many difficulties she had to face -- and by eight o'clock, she was so tired she could hardly get out of bed."

On the other hand, Henry David Thoreau used to lie in bed before rising and tell himself all the good news. When he arose, he was ready to meet the challenges before him.

Attitude is everything! It is well said that "we cannot direct the wind, but we can adjust our sails."

When you arise tomorrow morning, will you first adjust your sails?

P.S.

It is said that "the truly happy person is one who can enjoy the scenery while on detour." Be happy!

Our Greatest Songs Are Still Unsung!

Do you dread the future? Or will you warmly welcome it as you would a new friend?

Senator Hubert Humphrey, a man with an indomitable zest for living, once talked about the "good old days." He said, "They were never that good, believe me. The good new days are today, and better days are coming tomorrow. Our greatest songs are still unsung."

What a marvelous spirit! Our greatest songs are still unsung! Quite a different spirit is found in a business magazine ad that pictures a newborn baby with the caption: "Only 22,463 days until retirement." The ad is cute, but it picks up on a spirit of our day. It is a spirit of worry and anxiety. It is a spirit that tells us, "You don't know what the future holds! It is likely to be bleak; even disastrous! You can never be too careful!" You know what spirit I mean.

I have always believed in the future. And I will look forward to it with great anticipation. Why shouldn't I make friends with the future? After all, I intend to spend the rest of my life there!

I am intrigued by a story about a bishop back in the 1870s. The bishop had charge of a small denominational college. Annually, he visited the school and stayed in the home of the president.

The bishop was a narrow thinker with a dim view of the future. He told the school president during one of those visits that everything that could be invented had already been invented.

The administrator disagreed. "In 50 years," he contested, "people will learn to fly like birds."

That kind of talk greatly disturbed the bishop. "Flight is reserved for birds and angels," he said emphatically, "and you, sir, are guilty of blasphemy!"

The name of the bishop was Milton Wright. That name may not have a great deal of meaning to you, but something else will. You see, back at home, this clergyman had two enthusiastic sons -- Orville and Wilbur -- who believed that our greatest songs were still unsung! The rest of the story is one of an enthusiastic belief in tomorrow. You know how it ends.

Do you believe that your greatest songs are still unsung? Will you joyously welcome tomorrow, and all the tomorrows to come? Supported by those we hold dear and undergirded by faith, we, too, can share an enthusiastic belief in tomorrow!

No Great Talent

"I don't have any talent." You have certainly heard those words. You may have even said them yourself! And quite possibly, if you looked closely enough, you might discover that you are wrong.

Mary Frye enjoyed writing poetry. She wasn't interested in publishing her poems, and occasionally she passed one on to a friend who could use a lift. "I don't figure I have any great talent," the Baltimore, Maryland homemaker said. But many people would disagree. One of her poems, especially, has given hope and comfort to people who mourn for over 50 years.

When a friend of hers lost someone close, Mary Frye jotted down a poem, which seemed to spring from her heart, and gave it to the grieving woman. That poem was later passed on to others, who, in turn, passed it on until it became an American classic. "If it helps one person through a hard time, I am amply paid," said the poet, who has received no remuneration for her uncopyrighted work. It has been used in countless funeral services, translated and used in foreign lands and even incorporated into television drama.

Here is her original text, which has moved so many for so long:

Do not stand at my grave and weep,
I am not there, I do not sleep.

I am in a thousand winds that blow,
I am the softly falling snow.
I am the gentle showers of rain,
I am the fields of ripening grain.

I am in the morning hush,
I am in the graceful rush
Of beautiful birds in circling flight,
I am the starshine of the night.

I am in the flowers that bloom,
I am in a quiet room,
I am the birds that sing,
I am in each lovely thing.

Do not stand at my grave and cry,
I am not there. I do not die.

How many people are finding strength and solace from a verse jotted by a woman who always professed she had no talent? And what if she had kept her poetry to herself? Don't be afraid to use the talents you do possess, it has been well advised. The woods would be very silent if only the birds with the sweetest songs were heard.

Beauty Secret

Comic Phyllis Diller quipped that she once entered a beauty contest. "I not only came in last," she said, "I was hit in the mouth by Miss Congeniality."

Ed Feinhandler believes he is the world's ugliest man! But others disagree because, the fact is, Ed has discovered a universal "beauty secret."

He has won 15 "Ugly Man" competitions. According to the *Daily Sparks Tribune* (Sparks, Nevada USA), Ed drives a minivan with "Mr. Ugly" personalized license plates. Good looks were never important to him. But helping people always has been, and the thousands of dollars he has raised over the years from "Ugly Man" competitions has been donated to charity. In his spare time, Ed coaches youth sports, teaches tennis to underprivileged children and delivers Christmas baskets to the elderly. That's the beauty of it!

To know Ed is to know a beautiful man whose real attractiveness comes from within. His secret is that beauty has little to do with physical looks, and much to do with the heart.

You, too, probably know some exquisitely beautiful people. They are kind and generous. They are happy and contented. And if you look closely inside your own heart, you may discover more beauty there than you imagined possible. For as Ed Feinhandler teaches us, beauty has more to do with love than looks.

Joy Along the Way

A senator once took Will Rogers to the White House to meet President Coolidge. He warned the humorist that Coolidge never smiled. Rogers replied, "I'll make him smile." Inside the Oval Office, the senator introduced the two men.

"Will Rogers," he said, "I'd like you to meet President Coolidge."

Deadpan, Rogers quipped, "I'm sorry, but I didn't catch the name." Coolidge smiled.

A sense of humor is a marvelous gift to have. It is one of the most important means we possess to face the difficulties of life. And sometimes life can be difficult.

I deal professionally with issues which are critical: relationships breaking apart, people losing jobs, people facing serious illness or agonizing with someone close who is suffering, addictions, grief and heartache. Without a sense of humor about my own life, I don't know if I could survive! I take what I do seriously, but I try not to take myself too seriously. Like the New York City cab driver who said, "It's not the work that I enjoy so much, but the people I run into!"

151

Here is an experiment: look for and find as much joy as possible for one full day. Try to enjoy the people you run into, the work you do, your leisure time and your relationships. Don't forget to enjoy yourself -- and take enough time to enjoy God. Try this experiment for one full day, and by evening you will bask in the glow of a rekindled spirit.

It just takes a day to find joy along the way.

Index

Index, cont.